The Modern Nursing : its History and Development

The Modern Nursing: its History and Development

Based on the works of Abraham Jacobi; Ingleby Scott; David W. Clark.

History and Civilization Collection

LM Publishers

The development of sick-nursing is one of the most notable features of modern social life.

The evolution of the sick-nurse is mainly due to three very diverse influences—religion, war and science — to name them in chronological order.

It was religion which first induced ladies, in the earlier centuries of Christianity, to take up the care of the sick as a charitable duty. The earliest forerunner of the great sisterhood of nurses of whom we have any record was Fabiola, a patrician Roman lady, who in A.D. 380 founded a hospital in Rome with a convalescent home attached, and devoted herself and her fortune to the care of the sick poor. She had a rival in the empress Flaccilla, the pious consort of Theodosius I. (A.D. 379-395), who also personally visited the hospitals and attended on the sick.

The names of the oldest foundations which still survive, such as the Hôtel Dieu in Paris, St Thomas's and St Bartholomew's in London, the order of St Augustine, and (in the form of a modern revival) that of St John of Jerusalem, sufficiently indicate the original religious connection.

The credit of inaugurating the new order of things belongs to Germany, and here again the religious influence came into play. The beginning of the modern system dates from the foundation of the institute for training deaconesses at Kaiserswerth by Pastor Fliedner in 1836.

The Kaiserswerth Institute had a far-reaching and lasting influence, and may fairly claim to be the mother of the modern system. England, in particular, owes much to it, for there Florence Nightingale acquired the practical knowledge which enabled her afterwards to turn her remarkable gift of organization to such brilliant account. The example of Kaiserswerth was soon followed, and not in Germany only. In 1838 the Society of Friends founded a nursing organization in Philadelphia, and in 1840 Mrs Fry, a member of the same community, started the Institution of Nursing Sisters in London.

The training system, thus inaugurated on a semi-religious basis, received a new impetus from the Crimean War, which was further emphasized by the Civil War in America and the subsequent great conflicts on the continent. The despatch of Florence Nightingale with a staff of trained nurses, to superintend the administration of the military hospitals was the direct result of the publicity given to the details of the Crimean War by The Times, and it formed a new departure which riveted the eyes of the civilized world. The work undertaken and accomplished by this lady was far more important than the mere nursing of sick and wounded soldiers. She had grasped the principles of hygiene, which were then beginning to be understood, and she applied them to the reform of the hospital administration. In civil life it had a marked effect in stimulating the training movement and raising the status of the nurse; but substantial results were only obtained by degrees. It was not until 1860 that the modern hospital school system was definitely inaugurated by the opening of the Nightingale Fund School at St Thomas's Hospital, founded with the money subscribed by the British public in recognition of Miss Nightingale's national services, and worked on principles laid down by her.

(Encyclopedia Britannica, 1911)

Part 1

The Historical Development of Modern Nursing[1]

Nursing is as old as the human species. Even among animals, such as they are at present, we find occasional sympathy with fellow-suffering, and meet with efforts for the purpose of relief. We cannot imagine that human beings, in ever so remote prehistoric times, should have lived together, or near each other, without mutual attempts at relief, when suffering or sick. But this is presumption only, not history. No book, no tradition refers to facts in regard to the subject until the times of ancient Hellas and its successor in civilization, ancient Rome. Antiquity yields but few proofs of systematic nursing. It is true, hospitality was

---

[1] By Abraham Jacobi.

the pre-eminent virtue of the Greek. The stranger was always welcome. If he was sick, he was doubly so. In all Hellas poor sick citizens found ready admission to and nursing in the houses of the rich. It may be that the facility of finding private relief on the part of the sick was one of the causes why no systematic and collective efforts for the purpose of attending and nursing the sick were ever made to any extent. That such was the case, there can be little doubt; for the temples of Æsculapius and the adjoining residences of the physicians were probably not hospitals, but temporary domiciles for those who congregated in large numbers around the homes of the gods. Of the same nature was the edifice erected by Antoninus Pius near the temple of the Epidaurian Æsculapius.

In Italy, also, the temple of Æsculapius, on the island in the Tiber, between Rome and the outlet of the river, was never of much importance as a hospital or sanitarium. The only real hospitals at all comparable with institutions such as we have, existed in favor of human property, and for the benefit of soldiers. According to the testimony of Columella, Seneca, and Celsus, the Romans had hospitals for slaves, warriors, and gladiators. In Greece, also, as early as the period of Solon, those injured on the battle-field were attended and nursed at the expense of the community. Of the great Cæsar it is well known that he had a regular medical service in his armies.

There is a word in the ancient Greek which has given rise to the belief that Hellas may have had hospitals. But, as no facts and reports sustain that supposition, it is probable that ιατρειον meant a medical office, a policlinic, perhaps, but not a hospital. Real hospitals were not built by either Greek, Roman, or Hebrew. The commonwealth of the latter was hierarchic and intolerant. The stranger—though he who was permitted to live in Judea was to be treated like a member of the community—was to be exterminated, and must not be spared. Thus, while there are no proofs of the existence of hospitals for the friend, a painstaking care in favor of the stranger was out of the question.

Antiquity, however, is not without its humane culture. The reconciling feature in that immense picture of indifference and thoughtlessness is found in Buddhism.

We have the reliable report of a genuine hospital founded by a king in Ceylon, in the 5th century B. C. One of his successors in the

2nd century B. C. is credited with eighteen hospitals under regular medical superintendence. In the East Indies hospitals are mentioned in the third century. Nor have other civilizations been slow in outgrowing the humane exertions of Hellas, Rome, and Palestine, for Prescott tells us that there were hospitals in Mexico before the Christian Spaniards introduced the blessings of torture, inquisition, and extermination. And when finally the Christians, in the second century after Christ, bethought themselves of the poor and sick and established hospitals, the largest and most effective ones were founded in Asia Minor and Persia, where Buddhism had prepared both means and public opinion Buddhism, under whose beneficent rules aiding the poor and nursing the sick were two of the religious duties of kings and princes. Nor has Christianity the claim of having the first *large* hospitals. The Arabs had many good and large hospitals about 1200. Cordova, in Spain, sustained fifty within its own walls.

The first information in regard to Christian hospitals dates back to the second century; other reports go back as far as the fourth, and a few others to the sixth century. In most cases the establishments were not exactly hospitals, but stopping-places and dormitories for pilgrims on their way to Rome. To what extent such institutions were necessities is best proved by the order of the so-called "Bridge-makers" (*Hospitaliers Pontifes*), whose original vocation it was to protect pilgrims from the robberies and rapacity of the ferry-men on the large rivers. They existed a long time, became rich and degenerated, and were finally dissolved in 1672 by Louis XIV.

The hierarchic character of the institutions calculated to benefit the poor remained intact until the period of the Crusade wars. At that time Italian and German merchants initiated the great combinations of the several orders of Hospital Brothers.

Their efforts were not isolated or altogether premature. For there existed a humanistic movement among the better classes of the Occident, on a Christian basis it is true, but spontaneous. Particularly in the cities, societies were formed for the purpose of nursing the sick and aiding the forlorn. Guy, of Montpellier, France, established a hospital in that city, *of larger size*, while up to that time all the institutions of a similar character were small and unavailing, and located outside the walls. The new hospital in Montpellier, and seven more French houses, and two under the same direction in Rome, are first mentioned in a bull of Pope Innocent III, in the year 1198.

The secular character of the institutions was at that time fully recognized. In connecting four clergymen with them he commanded that they were to attend to spiritual duties only ("*sine contradictione et murmuratione*"), and not to interfere with the office of the superiors. In 1204 the same pope recognized the newly established Hospital of the Holy Ghost, on the old Tiber bridge, in Rome. With the peculiar mixture of ferocity and mildness so common to the mediæval age, the same man who humiliated emperors, dethroned kings, and persecuted the French heretics with fire and sword to extermination, looked for the helpless and sick in the streets and saved illegitimate babies from their watery graves. Guy de Montpellier's creation, the Order of the Holy Ghost, did not remain long in its original condition.

Pope Gregory X (1271-1276) subjected all the houses belonging to the order to the one located in Rome, the first step in the attempt at depriving the order and its hospitals of their secular supervision. It was finally disposed of by the bull of Pope Sixtus IV, of the 21st of March, 1477. Meanwhile and afterward the order spread over all Europe. With its increasing wealth and power it degenerated in the seventeenth century. Though clerical by name, it was the most secular of all the institutions of dissipation. Grand-master and officers lived on the fat of the land and their immense income. In vain Louis XIV attempted to abolish it. The only change French royalty could work was its transmutation into a royal order. In some of the provinces laymen had succeeded, however, in controlling the management. Thus it was in many parts of Germany, where, between 1400 and 1600, several of the institutions belonging to the order were secularized. In Italy, however, the Order of the Holy Ghost remained exclusively clerical. As late as in the beginning of the eighteenth century it had great possessions in Europe and the West Indies.

The Order of St. Elizabeth was founded in 1225 by Elizabeth, daughter of Andrew II of Hungary, and wife of Landgrave Ludwig of Thuringia. Women need not complain that domestic virtues do not warm more than their own home, and do not immortally challenge the admiration of posterity. Her name will never die, when many a great warrior's memory will be buried out of sight. She founded two hospitals in Eisenach, and another in Marburg, into which the twenty-two-years-old widow retired. The rule was to nurse the female sick only. But when Francis-Joseph and Windischgrätz (*par nobile fratrum*) let loose their Croats over unhappy Vienna, in our own times in 1848, the Sisters of St. Elizabeth were in the front ranks bringing aid and comfort.

In 1171 the orders of St. Protais and St. Gervais were founded in France. About the same time, the houses in Roncesvalles and Burgos. In 1409 José Gilaberto established an order in Valencia for the special purpose of nursing the lunatic.

Those I have mentioned, with several others, were orders founded by the Church, or whose supervision soon became clerical.

Those which, though all of them were anxious to submit to the Church, for spiritual reasons, succeeded in retaining their autonomy, must be credited with more real success in accomplishing their ends. Among the first we have any information of is the order of St. Catherine. Its members nursed poor and strange women and girls three days, and buried those who died in prisons or in the streets. In those good old times to which many dissatisfied hearts of today look back with longing eyes, those good olden times with their innocence, simplicity, and piety, this dying in the street was of common occurrence, and the Sisters of St. Catherine had plenty of work. We have not only accumulated seven more centuries, but gained more safety, more comfort, and more confidence in the future of mankind.

In the Hôtel-Dieu, the immense Paris hospital, thirty-eight men and thirty-eight women served as nurses. The places were, in later centuries, filled by Sisters of Mercy.

The Brothers of Mercy were founded in 1534 by Juan di Dios (John of God) in Granada. They were laymen, entered the order at between eighteen and thirty-one years of age, and nursed the sick of every faith and creed. Within a hundred years they possessed 18 hospitals, and there was a time when in Spain and the West Indies they had 138 hospitals, with 4,140 beds, and 47,000 sick annually, and in the rest of Europe 155 hospitals, 7,210 beds, and 150,000 sick. Twenty-five years ago they had in Austria alone 29 hospitals, with 20,000 patients.

Of similar character were the Obregons, founded about 1600, with their complicated duties of nursing the sick, praying, and repenting. This multitude of duties must have crippled their efficiency; they cannot compare with the Brothers of Mercy.

The "Bons Fils" (Good Boys) were founded in Flanders in 1615. They were tradesmen, with the duties of nursing the sick, mainly the alienated in their homes, and giving elementary instruction.

The Confraternita della Perseveranza was established in Rome, in 1663, for the purpose of caring for the strangers in the taverns.

The Order of the Sisters of Mercy was founded in 1617 by Vincent de Paul, a preacher. In a sermon he placed before his congregation the case of a poor and sick family, urging their co-operation and sympathy. Enthusiasm and much zeal were roused, and a noble and gifted woman, Louise de Marillac, the wife of Legras, the secretary of Mary of Medicis, enlisted herself at once in the service of that family and of many equally indigent. She and her friends worked both in private residences and in hospitals, and were soon recognized as an order. As early as 1636 a house was founded for the care and education of children and women, a foundling hospital was established, and a home for the alienated in 1645. Her order owned, after a single century, 290 stations, and had 1,500 members, who entered between the ages of eighteen and twenty-four, bound themselves for life to the order and the Church, and worked in hospitals and private residences, in the interest of both women and men, in rescuing fallen girls and educating the young.

In Rome, mainly in this century, they assisted those taken with infectious and acute diseases who could not be admitted to the public hospitals, and everywhere they attended the chronic cases of sickness of all denominations. Their foothold in Germany dates from this century only. Their greatest adversity was the all-purifying thunder-storm, the French Revolution. Many emigrated to England, but during the Napoleonic wars their services were so much appreciated as to procure for Sister Martha the cross of the Legion of Honor.

All of the orders mentioned were composed of Catholics. Not one of them but was intimately associated with the Church. In this connection it ought not to be forgotten that all the culture and knowledge of the mediaeval period was confined within the limits of the Church. Within its fold the whole progress of mankind, slow though it was, toward humanistic evolution, was developed. Thus the efforts of the Catholic Church in favor of the poor and sick must be duly appreciated, the more so, as the so-called "Reformation" party exhibits nothing but blank leaves in the history of ethical and humane development. The revolutionary movement prepared by powerful minds for centuries, and finally carried out by Luther, did not result in any good to the sick and poor for a long time. Indeed, the success of the Reformation was in part due to the greed of German princes, who gained a rich harvest by appropriating monasteries, hospitals, and all other possessions of the Catholic Church. Thus the Lutheran Church, or churches, were left so poor that if they *had* the will they had not the *power* to make any pecuniary sacrifices in the interest of the poor and sick. But *even that will* they had not, could not have. For the first axiom in Luther's doctrine was this, that *not work performed, but faith only*, made the Christian. That doctrine was a long stride backward; it fired the imagination of some bigots, chilled the hearts of most men, sustained the egotist, and created dissensions. Never was there a greater failure. The poetry of the Church gone, its efficiency gone, that was the "reformation." Not until some decades ago did we know of Protestant unions established on the plan of their Catholic predecessors. But the *male* orders never tried to imitate the useful example of the Catholics. *They* did not care for the sick or the poor. *Their aim* was and is "home-mission." *They* are replete with faith, distribute Bibles, and glory in the conversion of that Jew who was baptized, once or often, half a dozen years ago, for ready cash.

The women, as always, have done better. Their hospital orders, mainly the Deaconesses, have done good work this half-century, both in public institutions and in private. During the war-times in Germany they and other associations established on similar plans did good work, and deserve all the praise bestowed upon them. Their recognition was complete. Princesses joined hands with them — the Archduchess of Baden, Princess Alice of Darmstadt, the Empress Augusta. And not only in military hospitals did they earn deserved praise. Some general hospitals, such as the Augusta Hospital in Berlin, derive great benefit from their incessant and intelligent labors. I do not mean to stint praise, and therefore make this statement of their work, which has been performed under apparently great difficulties. These difficulties are the very rules, for instance, of the Deaconesses of Kaiserwerth, from which I quote for your edification the following introductory paragraph:

"The Christian women who wish to undertake the office of a nursing sister, as deaconess for the sick and poor, must possess a somewhat advanced Christian knowledge. Mere church-membership, mere attendance on Christian assemblies, and reading of Christian works of edification, are not enough. The love of reading the word of God, and a diligent use of the same for a long time past, must exist, as well as a knowledge of the more important histories of the Old and New Testaments. There must also be a knowledge of the sinful heart from their own personal experience, as well as experience of the grace of Christ, in order that they may have learned to despair of themselves, and in their weakness to trust only to the strength of Christ. A Christian walk of life must for a long time have adorned such Christian women," and so on, and so on. You will admit that in the face of so much hyper-religious sentiment an active, unselfish, modern woman must feel bewildered.

After all I have said, it is evident that the cause of humanity was originally not hampered by the efforts of the Catholic Church. On the contrary, many centuries ago it was the only safe deposit, inasmuch as the Arabs lost their importance in humanistic evolution from the fourteenth century, for the gradual development of human feeling. But that human feeling was not fostered and protected because it was human; the Church had but one purpose, the aggrandizement of the Church. The latter has a meaning in the case of the Catholic Church, which is at least a union, and has a uniform standard, which Protestantism never had and never can have.

The latter has, in its imitation of the ways and words of the mediæval rules of Catholic orders, proved one truth, and I emphasize that because here is the great difference between church nursing and modern nursing. "Clerical care of the sick is destined, under the rules, to serve the Church, whatever that may mean, while serving the sick; the main duties and aims in view are ecclesiastical, and not humane, and, instead of a nurse solely given to the performance of her duties, you deal with ecclesiastical officers" (Virchow). And the necessity is clear, that whatever organization is deemed advisable in the interest of the sick, that organization ought to be in our times unecclesiastical and unsectarian. I have alluded to the fact that whatever medical knowledge existed in the masses centuries ago did so through the medium of the clergy. That knowledge was but trifling, for the ancient medicine of the Greeks and the more recent labors of the Arabs were sealed books at that time. But, then, the clergyman was the doctor. Instead of being so at present, we are daily met with the fact that the exact tendency of modern medicine is an unknown territory to the clergy, and that among them the upholders of all sorts of doubtful practices find their most sincere supporters. Medicine is to them a matter of faith, not science. It is not necessary to refer to that Brooklyn impostor whose criminal career has been detailed but lately in the secular press. For no church and no denomination must be held responsible for his methods of fleecing the ignorant and credulous. But the instances where actual clergymen assume responsibilities beyond their clerical powers and duties are also very numerous, and the protection by the Church of a regular monk in a Jersey monastery, who, in the church of his own institution, plies his nefarious trade of laying on hands, and exorcising the devils of disease for cash, these ten years, proves to what extent faith can be abused and the essence of religion distorted. We still live in a time when mediæval ignorance and modern enlightenment appear to find resting-places side by side. That the latter is getting the upper hand, after all, this sketch will prove, I hope, for even the mediæval organizations in the interest of the poor and sick, which I was anxious to estimate at their full value, have finally failed ignominiously. Almost every large society of the kind would degenerate in the end. The uniform report concerning most of them, mainly the male orders, is this, that with increasing power and wealth the original unselfishness of the founder disappeared, the actual work was left to low servants, the wealth of the community was accumulated in the Church. Thus it was that every great calamity sweeping over the lands was a source of riches to the Church. Never was divine blessing more visible in the Church than when half the population of Europe succumbed under the destruction of the "black-death." Never was more business shrewdness developed by "fathers" and "brothers" than when a patient, sick with leprosy—much less contagious than was made out by those who had an interest in exaggerating its dangers—had to give up half his property before being permitted to bury himself for life in the out-of-town places provided by the Church. The omnivorous taste and good digestion of the Church have become proverbial.

The majority of the clerical associations having failed, the seventeenth and still more the eighteenth centuries were far behind former periods in regard to systematic nursing. It has taken a long time between the church institutions, which no longer came up to the intentions of their founders, and the spontaneous efforts of free men and women who felt the necessity of appropriate efforts on a different basis. The history of this slow evolution is very interesting; it is the co-ordinate of the history of a healthy and wholesome individualism in general, after long indifference and chaos.

Schools for training nurses were established in Germany fifty years ago; in Berlin by Dieffenbach, Kluge, and Gedike, and in Göttingen by Ruhstaat. Books to serve the purpose of instructing nurses and the public in general have been written by numerous men and women, some of them, particularly in our days, by celebrities. Gedike himself published a work, fifty years ago, which is a very readable one even now. Passing by Nightingale[2], who has proved how to become immortal without enjoying high office, or playing on cannon, or tyrannizing nations, or being borne on a throne, let me allude to but a few illustrious names: Nothnagel, who wrote on the nursing of those sick with nerve-diseases; Billroth, who published a book on nursing

---

[2] The second part of this book will treat of Florence Nightingale and her role in the founding of the modern nursing.

in general; Esmarch, who taught the first aid in emergencies; and the greatest of the many great men of the century, Virchow, with his many contributions to the literature of the subject, and mainly, in 1869, with a lecture "On the Instruction of Women in caring for the Sick outside the existing Ecclesiastical Organizations."

This instruction of women in caring for the sick, and the relation of women to nursing as a profession, can be considered from two distinct points of view: first, in its influence upon them; second, in its effects upon the public.

The first consideration is a very important one. The opposition to women stepping out of their sphere, which was meant to be cooking and washing, knitting and darning, begging alms and taking a daily whipping, also getting married and raising a family, has been overcome by common sense and habit. Common sense ceased to understand why or how every woman could or should cook and wash, knit and darn, beg alms, or get whipped or married. And habits are formed and reformed with such rapidity that opposition becomes changed into favor in a few years. It is but little more than a dozen years since women physicians were recognized by the profession; not over half a dozen years since you heard of women lawyers. The female part, and, for that matter, the male part of my audience also, are sorry they heard so much of a woman lawyer in a Western town. At all events, the opposition to the attempt at widening woman's sphere, or spheres, has ceased, and the recognition of the principles of equal rights, no matter for what color or sex, or previous servitude, is all but universal.

You will not care to go into the question now, whether law or medicine will ever he resorted to by women to any great extent. The entire liberty given them has proved already, will prove more in future, that neither law nor medicine is an appropriate vocation for any but an exceptional class of women, and that the opposition to women practitioners of law and medicine will come less from the professions than from the public. For the public will never admit that a person in the practice of a profession should not give his or her entire attention and strength to it, and the women of the country will never admit that the superintendence of a home and the proper raising of a family are not sufficient employments of all the time and all the powers of the most gifted woman.

The amateurs are losing ground. Thus it is that the professions will never be overrun, and the fear of undue competition has long died out, even among the most chicken-hearted braves of the professions. But the question is not how many women will avail themselves of the opportunities granted, but whether they shall have those opportunities, and whether these shall be given the women of all walks of life, of all standards of intellect. And the question has generally been answered affirmatively, to such an extent that it is considered self-understood that, while the mediæval ages attempted to help them as much as possible, modern times prefer to give them the power to help themselves. In regard to nursing, attention was called early to the unmarried and poor among the women.

The statistics of Berlin, of the year 1872, proved that every third woman had to provide for herself. It was remarked with surprise that, of 407 such helpless and breadless creatures, but a single one went into nursing as a business. In other Continental cities it was still worse. In Vienna the shiftlessness of women was still greater; misery and poverty reigned supreme, as must be expected when you learn that a woman who took the making of her own clothing, even *with the aid* of a professional seamstress, into her own hands was punishable under the law.

The proportion of but one nurse to 407 women, who had to work for a living, is remarkable, it is true. For are not nursing, and caring, and attending implanted in woman's nature? What is the reason that so few went into nursing as a business, if not a vocation? Probably, because the women felt, or the public made them feel, that without careful preparation no nurse, or *soi-disant* nurse, can be efficient. We have still the remnants, I fear numerous ones, of that self-made class of nurses among us. In my own recollection of far-away years I remember a great many, and a great many, I was told but lately, remember me also, perhaps too well. Some of you may have seen them—in other people's houses—wrinkled prematurely, thinned out by temper, contrary by nature, or for the most part fattened in the course of their (to them) useful career, complacent, and drowsy while everything was going well, incompetent and snappish when danger required work and sufficiency, always ready to have their regular meals served up-stairs by the help of the house, who breathed freely when they finally left, and always willing to spend their time between rocking a baby, speaking of their long experience, sleeping ten hours, talking gossip all day long, and drinking eleven cups of coffee in the twenty-four hours. This is hardly an exaggeration, for the number of women who took up nursing as a business, driven to it by some natural disposition, gifted with some intellect, modest and willing to profit by superior knowledge and experience, interested in the welfare of their patients, and never stunted in their human feelings by the force of habit, was rather small. But I am glad to say I knew such, too. I gladly shook their hands when I happened to meet them on a common errand, gladly recognizing the diploma they carried in their brains and hearts. But these exceptions proved the rule, and the rule conveyed no blessing. It was, it is, a sad fact that nursing all over the world grew worse in just the same time when medical science grew more exact and medical practice more effective.

Relief in this city came none too soon. The president has detailed to you the history of the training-schools of New York. Since their time the practice in hospitals and in private dwellings has changed wonderfully. After thirty years' work in the city, after twenty-five years' constant labor in public institutions, I ought to know the difference. And I do know and publicly proclaim that the results of the best of physicians have vastly improved since their cases have been in the hands of trained nurses. This is so in private dwellings; it is the same in hospitals. In the hospitals the difference can be measured on a large scale. In them the trained nurse has worked a vast improvement.

Every large hospital ought to perform a double duty. It must give the poor patient, and many rich also, the best possible chance of recovery from sickness. It can afford to accomplish that, because of its pecuniary and intellectual means. Though a hospital be poor, there ought to be, there generally are, means enough to fill all the necessities required. And the intellectual means are expected, are supposed to be, above the average of the general practitioner. There are a great many reasons why that should be so, why hospital places should be open for the competition of the best material among the medical profession, recognized to be the best by the medical profession itself, and why family and personal influence should not fill places which are better not filled at all than with indifferent or bad material. A hospital must also grant the best possible nursing—attached, wakeful, careful. All this is due to the single patients.

A good deal more, however, is due to the public at large. A hospital looking for the interest of the single patient only might just as well be a private institution, a *maison de santé* for the benefit of a landlord. The benefit derived from hospital treatment by a sick person is not all the satisfaction due to a public who pay four hundred dollars a year for every bed. Nor are the public paid sufficiently for their sacrifices by the accumulated experiences of a few physicians, who enjoy the large field of observation and the opportunity of utilizing it for the benefit of private patients. Every hospital which neglects to increase the stock of medical knowledge, and to give an opportunity of learning the theory and practice of nursing and caring for the sick, performs its duties but half, and serves the public but incompletely. Every large hospital must be, and will be, a clinical school, and a school for nurses. It will be acknowledged that as the presence of a nurse in a sick-ward, who is sent there to learn, is considered unobjectionable, the presence of a few physicians observing a case, which cannot be injured by their so doing, is not only not injurious, but ought to be demanded by the public, who have a right to expect a physician in their own families who has seen and knows and understands what he is called in to treat. I do not see why hospital patients only should have the best money and service can afford, and why the public at large should have to fall back in many cases on untried skill. Thus the people have a right to demand that every large hospital should have a clinical school, and a training-school for nurses. The public, who are willing to pay for it, may also demand that the expenses of the same, particularly the nurses' school, should be borne by the hospital. This demand, if considered theoretical only, must stand as long as a hospital is, or claims to be, a public institution. When the board of directors of any institution will recognize that they are not the administrators of the dollars of a small concern, but the benefactors of the public at large, they will also appreciate not only that a few disinterested ladies will open their pocket-books, and collect voluntary contributions, but that a generous public will pay more willingly and more largely.

The demand that a large hospital should be a clinical school and a school for nurses, and that the expense should or might be borne by the institution, is not valid in the case of city or commonwealth hospitals only. Most of the hospitals of the country are originally private institutions. They obtain the character of being public affairs when an always increasing number of men and women become interested in and contributors to them. An institution with one or two thousand paying members represents ten or twenty thousand families — in fact, represents a city. And what it represents, of that it assumes the rights and duties. And the main duty the public at large will soon know how to enforce from the directors of every large hospital is, to administer the public domain to the greatest possible advantage for the greatest possible number.

The selfishness of an individual adversary, the animosity of evil-spirited persons will never weigh, ought never to weigh, against the public good; the latter only is the object of those who are placed in trust of money, institutions, and the public welfare, because of their actual or supposed public spiritedness and superior intellect.

Is it necessary to detail the advantages of the services of a trained nurse over those of an untrained one? The latter class, as a rule, brings to their work no previous education, no theoretical schooling, no technical experience. They come mostly from inferior walks of life, with less intellectual power, and less moral force. Only those who come from better stock, and raise themselves to higher ambitions, will spend money, and two years of their lives, for the purpose of learning both theoretically and practically the art of relieving the sick, aiding their comfort, taking responsibilities which sometimes are as difficult as they are life-saving, and obeying orders with intelligence and understanding. That such persons are valuable additions to our hygienic requirements and sanitary progress everybody can conceive. That without them many a case would not recover, in spite of the most competent medical skill, all of you may have experienced. I, for one, know from personal experience that many a case can be, has been saved, first by the medical orders; secondly, and often mostly, by the execution of orders, such an execution as is rendered possible by combined knowledge and skill only. If I say that we practitioners have commenced to feel safe in regard to many of our cases only since we could rely on the co-operation of a trained nurse, I express but a common observation. I trust that there are households within hearing which know how to appreciate the services rendered them by a trained nurse.

So much only in regard to individual cases. But the service to the public at large hitherto rendered, and constantly increasing, is of a different and still more important nature. Who is nowadays the teacher of the public at large in sanitary matters, in hygienic rules? The knowledge of the Church, when *it* nursed, was faith, and, let us add, in its best times, love. The knowledge of uneducated women was, and is, ignorance driven to actual or alleged work by starvation. The knowledge of a trained nurse is the result of a two years' study under competent teachers, and a constant practice. Who in the community is her superior in the knowledge of the facts mostly necessary for the health and life of your children, and dear ones in general? The clergyman is no longer the teacher of the mysteries of life and common sense. The schoolmaster or schoolmistress knows about the classics, geography, and arithmetic, but no normal school ever taught them the elements of applied physiology. The educated member of any profession except the medical has not the slightest idea of the necessities of the body, the action of food, the effect of clothing, and the hundred facts required by different ages, conditions, and states of health. With the exception of the physician, whose advice is frequently sought only to repair the effects of ignorance, the only teacher the public have, and will have, is *the trained nurse*. Ten or twenty families may enjoy her presence annually, ten or twenty mothers will learn simple and important truths, knowledge will increase, and prevention of disease will become a possibility. Enjoyable and useful as the service of a trained nurse is in an individual case of sickness, her services to the community are very much greater, by virtue of her theoretical and practical teaching. May I tell you what a good trained nurse may teach, and can teach? How to recognize a fever, how to compare the local temperatures of the several parts of the body, and how to equalize them; she knows that ever so many feeble children might have been saved, if but the feet and legs had not been allowed to get cold; how to bathe, when, and when to stop; how to regulate the position of the head — I remember quite well the case of inflammatory delirium which would always be relieved by propping up the head — how to treat intelligently an attack of fainting; how to render cow's milk digestible by repeated boiling, or lime-water, or table-salt, or farinaceous admixtures; how to feed in case of diarrhœa; how to refuse food in case of vomiting; how to apply and when to remove cold to the head; how to ventilate a room without draught; and a thousand other things. She will also use her knowledge and influence in weaning the public of nostrums, concerning which hardly anything is known except what you have to pay for the promises of the label. She will break the public of the indiscriminate use of quinia, with its dangers possibly for life; cure you of the tendency of making the diagnosis of malaria the scapegoat of every unfinished or impossible diagnosis; she will teach you that the frequent and reckless domestic use of chlorate of potassium leads to many a case of ailment, to chronic poisoning, possibly in the shape of Bright's disease or to acute poisoning with unavoidable death. These are but very few of the things she can do, and but a little of the knowledge she cannot but distribute. With the aid of the class of women who frequent our training-schools, the public at large must and will gain, in a short time. Let the number of the schools increase, and increase the number of pupils, and every one of them will be a teacher and an apostle of sound information on sanitary and hygienic subjects. And let nobody leave this place to-night without intending to aid an institution as helpful as this.

Will the pupils come? Certainly they will. There is an increasing demand for their services. Many times had I to wait a day or two before any of the schools could accommodate me. There is no fear that there ever will be too many good nurses. There is fear, either, that many persons of inferior intelligence and morals will present themselves for or obtain admission to a school. By attending the suffering, it is true, many a crude or brutal nature is ennobled; but I should not advise to run the risk of admitting that class at the expense of the sick, or of a rising and beneficent profession. The occasional specimens of cold-hearted and arrogant persons one is apt to meet, even among trained nurses, must discourage the admission of any but the very best. These will apply. The calling is an honorable one, it promises a competence, it corresponds with the innermost nature of woman. It is not true that the Church alone could raise the enthusiasm for hard work, the performance of arduous duties, and self-sacrifice. One of the first nurses I had in my division in Bellevue Hospital, many years ago, was an accomplished girl, the daughter of a rich man in the far West. After a year and a half it took all the influence and begging of her family to take her away from us and her hard work among the poorest of the poor.

The large number of ladies, wealthy and accomplished, who work assiduously and regularly under Felix Adler, and in other places, under our very eyes, prove that the very best class of society can be prevailed upon to do the hardest and most beneficent kind of work. And the fact that the elite of the women of the city are willing and anxious to undertake the arduous task of founding and supporting training-schools, in the face of all sorts of difficulties, proves also that the work is in accordance with the requirements of both woman's nature and humanity. There will be many trained nurses who will work for humanity's sake, as centuries ago they claimed to serve for God's sake. Many a woman who would have buried herself in a monastery centuries ago, driven from the face of the living earth by misunderstood and unsatisfied longing, I believe, would nowadays become a nurse, knowing and enthusiastic.

Ladies of the graduating class: The remarks I was expected to make have extended into a lecture. You have been used to lectures, however; if you had not enjoyed them, and profited by them, you would not be here to-night, the most honored and most conspicuous of this assembly. Thus I thought I might be permitted to speak, instead of to you, of you, and your chosen calling and its history. From nothing can any profession derive so much advantage as from the history of its development. It is certainly an interesting spectacle to see how your profession depended intimately on the changing conditions of thought and feeling among mankind. You are happy enough to live and work in a time when, while following individual tastes and having individual motives, your labors are given to the suffering for no outside reason, no church command, but from the free choice of free women in the interest of humanity. I had also to allude to several subjects which may to some appear a little outside the legitimate domain of your ambition and duties. You know better. An intelligent woman will not spend two of her young years in acquiring a certain knowledge without enlarging her horizon in general. You have chosen a profession as noble and as deserving as any there is in existence. You will be the interpreter's and right hands of the physician, and the connecting link between the physician and not only the single patient, but also the public at large.

My opinion of the services you can render is high, but I trust not exaggerated. When your numbers shall increase, and the character of those who are admitted remain of the same standard, your importance will grow. In your hands will, to a great extent, lie the opportunity for removing prejudices, spreading knowledge, healing and preventing disease. Even those of you who will not always consent to serve in *other* people's homes, will, by example and by teaching, remain in close alliance and co-operation with such as intend to remain in the ranks forever. As you now mean to leave us, endowed with the certificate of the required accomplishments, I can only add, while offering my best wishes for your future, that I trust you will never forget the place which gave you so ample opportunities for perfecting yourselves.

You will never forget the gentlemen who taught you, nor that accomplished young woman who impressed all of you with the fact that the charms of womanhood will not suffer from hard work, from a classical education, and thorough medical or other knowledge. Do not forget, also, at the beginning of your independent career, the ladies to whose care and sacrifices and labors you owe the existence of the school which sends you forth as its first graduates, nor the great charitable institution which, after having given you your practical training, honors you tonight by the presence of many of its officers, and designates its president to deliver to you your diplomas.

Part II

The Founding of Modern Nursing : the Story of Florence Nightingale

Florence Nightingale is considered as the founder of the modern nursing.

She was recognized as the leading expert upon all the questions involved; her advice flowed unceasingly and in all directions, so that there is no great hospital today which does not bear upon it the impress of her mind.

I [3]

Florence Nightingale will be, through all time, the representative nurse *by excellence*. One of the brightest, noblest names in the list of brave, heroic women.

In her case it is a special calling, in virtue of natural capacity, moral and intellectual at once. She did not set out from any chosen starting point. She did not propose to earn her own salvation by a life of good works. She was not incited by visions of a religious life in a favored monastic community. She did not aspire to take in hand a department of human misery, in order to extinguish it, and then look about to see what particular misery it should be. She does not appear to have had any plans relating to herself at all. Nor was she overtaken by the plague in a

---

[3] Based on Ingleby Scott.

village; nor did she overtake a fever in a village in the course of her travels, like her representative sisters of an earlier time; nor did she do the work of the occasion, and reenter ordinary life as if nothing had happened. Her case is special and singular in every way.

Her childhood and youth where very much like those of little girls who have wealthy parents, and carefully chosen governesses, and good masters, and much travel — in short, all facilities for intellectual cultivation by study and extended intercourse with society, at home and abroad.

The peculiarity in the case of herself and her nearest relatives seems to be their having been reared in an atmosphere of sincerity and freedom, — of reality, in fact, — which is more difficult to obtain than might be thought. There was a certain force and sincerity of character in the elder members on both sides of the house which could not but affect the formation of the children's characters; and in this case there was a governess also whose lofty rectitude and immaculate truthfulness commanded the reverence of all who knew her.

In childhood a domestic incident disclosed to the honest-minded little girl what her liking was, and she followed the lead of her natural taste. She took care of all cuts and bruises, and nursed all illness within her reach; and there is always a good deal of these things within the reach of country gentry who are wealthy and benevolent. For the usual term of young-lady life, Florence Nightingale did as other young ladies. She saw Italy, and looked at its monuments; she once went to Egypt and

Greece with the Bracebridges; she visited in society, and went to court. But her heart was not in the apparent objects of her life — not in travel for amusement, nor in art. In literature, books which disclosed life and its miseries, and character with its sufferings, burnt themselves in upon her mind, and created much of her future effort. She was never resorted to for sentiment. Sentimentalists never had a chance with her. Besides that her character was too strong, and its quality too real, for any sympathy with shallowness and egotism, she had two characteristics which might well daunt the sentimentalists — her reserve, and her capacity for ridicule. Ill would they have fared who had come to her for responsive sympathies about sentiment, or even real woes in which no practical help was proposed; and there is perhaps nothing uttered by her, from her evidence before the Sanitary Commission for the Army to her recently published "Notes on Nursing," which does not disclose powers of irony which self-regardant persons may well dread.

Such force and earnestness must find or make a career. She evidently believes, as all persons of genius do, that she found it, while others say she made it. Philosophy will hereafter reconcile the two in her case and many others. As a matter of fact, while other young ladies were busy, and perhaps better employed than usual, in enjoying the great exhibition, she was in the Kaiserwerth Institution, on the Rhine, going through the training for nursing, and investigating the methods of organization there and elsewhere.

The strongest sensation she perhaps ever excited among her personal acquaintance was when she undertook to set up the Sanitarium in Harley Street, and left home to superintend the establishment. Her first work there was chiefly financial; and the powers of administration she manifested were a complete justification of what she had done in leaving her father's house to become what people called the matron of a charity. At first common-minded people held up hands and eyes as if she had done something almost scandalous. Between that day and this they must have discovered that she could exalt any function, and that no function could lower her. She rectified the accounts, paid the debts, and brought all round; and she always had leisure to help and comfort the sick ladies in the house. At one time, I remember, there was not a case in the house which was not hopeless; but there was no sign of dismay in Florence Nightingale. She completed her task, showing unconsciously by it how a woman as well as a man may be born to administration and command.

By a sort of treachery only too common in the visitors of celebrated people, we have all seen the letter of Mr. Sidney Herbert, in 1854, entreating Miss Nightingale to go — accompanied by her friends the Bracebridges, who are familiar with life in the East — to Turkey, to minister among the sick and wounded of our array. How soon she was ready, and how she and her band of nurses went, and were just in time to receive the wounded from Inkermann, no Englishman forgets. No man of any nation concerned will ever forget her subsequent services. She had against her not only a chaos of disorder in which to move, and a hell of misery around her to relieve, but special difficulties in the jealousy of the medical officers, the rawness of the nurses so hastily collected, and the incompatibilities of the volunteer ladies who started on the enterprise with her or after her. On the state of the hospitals it can, I hope, never be necessary to enlarge again. We all know how, under her superintendence, places became clean and airy, and persons cleanly, clothed, fed, and afforded some chance of recovery from maladies or wounds. "While history abides, the image of Florence Nightingale, lamp in hand, going through miles of beds, night by night, noting every patient as she went, and ministering wherever most wanted, will always glow in men's hearts; and the sayings of the men about her will be traditions for future generations to enjoy.

She was prostrated by the Crimean fever at Balaklava, and carried up to the hospital on the cliff's till she began to mend. When she was taken to sea. She would not come home, because her work at Scutari was not finished. She remained there till the end of the war; by which time she and her military and medical coadjutors had shown what hospitals may be, and how low the rate of mortality of an army may be reduced, even in time of war.

She has never recovered from that fever; and for some years she has been confined by severe and increasing illness. Not the less has she worked, steadily and most efficiently. She cannot fulfill her aim — of training nurses in an institution of her own, and thus raising up a body of successors.

The grateful people of England supplied the means, "without her knowledge or desire, which was the same thing as imposing a new service upon her. She wished to decline it when she found how little likely her health was to improve. Her letter to the trustees of the fund must be fresh in all memories, and the reply of the trustees, who satisfied her that the money was accumulating, and the plan and the public able and willing to wait. If she could not do this particular work, she has done many others. Her written evidence before the Sanitary Commission for the Army is a great work in itself. So are various reforms urged on the military authorities by her and her coadjutors, and now adopted by the war office. Reforms in the Indian army are about to follow. The lives thus saved no one will attempt to number; and the amount of misery and vice precluded by her scientific humanity is past all estimate.

Her "Notes on Nursing," prepared and issued in illness and pain, are the crowning evidence of what she is, and can do. Hitherto we have, I trust, appreciated and honored her acts; now we are enabled to perceive and appreciate her mind. It was as certain before as it can ever be that she must have acquired no little science, in various departments, to produce the effects she wrought; but we see it all now.

We see also, much more clearly than ever, her moral characteristics. I will not describe them when they can be so much better seen in her "Notes on Nursing." Anyone who reads those Notes without being moved in the depths of his heart will not understand the writer of them by any amount of description; and those who have been so moved do not need and will not tolerate it. The intense and exquisite humanity to the sick, underlying the glorious common sense about affairs, and the stern insight into the weaknesses and the perversions of the healthy, troubled as they are by the sight of suffering, and sympathizing with themselves instead of the patient, lay open a good deal of the secret of this wonderful woman's life and power. We begin to see how a woman, anything but robust at any time, may have been able, as well as willing, to undertake whatever was most repulsive and most agonizing in the care of wounded soldiers and crowds of cholera patients. We see how her minute economy and attention to the smallest details are reconcilable with the magnitude of her administration, and the comprehensiveness of her plans for hospital establishments, and for the reduction of the national rate of mortality. As the lives of the sick hang on small things, she is as earnest about the quality of a cup of arrowroot, and the opening and shutting of doors, as about the institution of a service between the commissariat and the regimental, which shall insure an army against being starved when within reach of food. In the mind of a true nurse nothing is too great or too small to be attended to with all diligence; and therefore we have seen Florence Nightingale doing and insisting upon the right about shirts and towels, spoon-meats, and the boiling of rice, and largely aiding in reducing the mortality of the army from nineteen in the thousand to eight, in times of peace.

In the spirit and tone of this book we see, too, how it is that, with all her fame, we have known so little of the woman herself. Where it is of use to tell any piece of her own experience, she tells it; and these scraps of autobiography will be eagerly seized upon by all kinds of readers; but, except for the purpose of direct utility, she never speaks of herself, more or less, or even discloses any of her opinions, views, or feelings. This reserve is a great distinction in these days of self-exposure, and descanting on personal experiences. It is the least possible rebuke to the egotism, or the sentimentality, which has led several ladies to imagine that they could be nurses, without having tried whether they could bear the discipline. Her pure, undisguised common sense, and her keen perception of all deviations from common sense, may have turned back more or fewer women from the nursing vocation; but this is probably an unmixed good; for those who could be thus turned back were obviously unfit to proceed. She is the representative of those only who are nurses; that is, capable of the hardest and highest duties and sacrifices which women can undertake from love to their race.

In the end she will have won over far more than she can have (most righteously and mercifully) discouraged. Generations of women for centuries to come will be the better, the more helpful, and the more devoted for Florence Nightingale having lived; and no small number of each generation will try their strength on that difficult path of beneficence which she has opened, and on which her image will forever stand to show the way.

Portrait of Florence Nightingale : An Angel of Mercy [4]

> Florence Nightingale, by her role in the development of the modern nursing gives us hope of our humanity, even in its darkest and most forbidding forms.

The scenes of the Crimean war in 1854 and 1855 are thus relieved by the heroic and philanthropic devotion of one whose name will live, enrolled upon the bright page of the world's benefactors, long after the illustrious generals who led in the conflict have been forgotten. The death-defying charge upon the field of Balaklava has not more certainly become "storied" in the world's history than have the philanthropy and heroism of Florence Nightingale.

---

[4] Based on the work of David W. Clark.

Miss Nightingale was a young lady of singular endowments, both natural and acquired. She early acquired a knowledge of the ancient languages, and of the higher branches of mathematics; while her attainments in general art, science, and literature were of no common order. Her command of modern languages was extensive, and she spoke French, German, and Italian fluently as her native English. She has visited and studied the various nations of Europe, and has ascended the Nile to its farthest cataract. While in Egypt she tended the sick Arabs with whom she came in contact; and it was frequently in her power, by judicious advice, to render them important services. Graceful, feminine, rich, and popular, her influence over those with whom she came in contact was powerful as it was gentle and persuasive. Her friends and acquaintances embraced a large circle, and included persons of all classes and persuasions; but her happiest place has ever been her home, where, in the center of numerous and distinguished relatives, and in the simplest obedience to her admiring parents, she dwelt.

Her personal appearance is described by Mr. Trenery in his Crescent City, as he saw her engaged in her mission of mercy. He says she is one of those whom God forms for great ends. You cannot hear her say a few sentences, nor even look at her, without feeling that she is an extraordinary being. Simple, intellectual, sweet, full of love and benevolence, innocent — she is a fascinating and perfect woman. She is tall and pale. Her face is exceedingly lovely; but better than all is the soul's glory that shines through every feature so exultingly. Nothing can be sweeter than her smile. It is like a sunny day in Summer; and more of holiness than is expressed in her countenance one does not often meet on a human face as one passes along the dusty highways of life. Through all her movements breathes that high intellectual calm which is God's own patent of nobility, and is the true seal of the most glorious aristocracy—that of mind, of soul!

From infancy she had a yearning affection for her kind—a sympathy with the weak, the oppressed, the destitute, the suffering, and the desolate. The schools and the poor around Lea Hurst and Embley first saw and felt her as a visitor, teacher, consoler, and expounder. Then she frequented and studied the schools, hospitals, and reformatory institutions of London, Edinburgh, and the continent. It appears by her evidence lately given before the English Army Medical Reform Commission, that she has devoted her attention to the organization of hospitals for thirteen years, during which time she has visited all the hospitals of London, Edinburgh, and Dublin; many country infirmaries, and some of the military and naval hospitals in England; all the hospitals in Paris, where she studied with the Sisters of Charity; the institution of the Protestant Deaconesses at Kaiserwerth, on the Rhine, where she was twice in training as a nurse; the hospitals at Berlin, and many others in Germany, and at Lyons, Brussels, Rome, Constantinople, and Alexandria; and the war hospitals of the French and Sardinians. Soon after her return home from the continent, the hospital established in London for sick governesses was about to fail for want of proper management, and Miss Nightingale consented to be placed at its head. Derbyshire and Hampshire were exchanged for the narrow, dreary establishment in Harley-street, to which she devoted the whole of her time and her fortune. While her friends missed her at assemblies, lectures, concerts, exhibitions, and all the entertainments for taste and intellect with which London in its season abounds, she whose powers could have best appreciated them was sitting beside the bed and soothing the last complaints of some poor, dying, homeless, hapless governess. Miss Nightingale found pleasure in tending these poor, destitute women in their infirmities, their sorrows, their deaths, or their recoveries. She was seldom seen out of the walls of the institution; and the few friends whom she admitted found her in the midst of nurses, letters, prescriptions, accounts, and interruptions. Her health sunk under the heavy pressure. Thus it appears she had received a special training for the great work to which she was providentially called.

When the accounts of the sufferings of the soldiery in the Crimea, of the additional rigors that they were enduring from want of effectual hospital treatment, and from defective management in supplying stores and necessary relief, she kindled at once with an enthusiastic desire to remedy the evil. The extent of that evil may be gathered from the first that there was, in the first seven months of the Crimean campaign, a mortality among the troops of sixty per cent. per annum from disease alone—a rate which exceeds that of the great plague of London, and a higher ratio than the mortality in cholera to the attacks. One of the chief points in which the deficiency of proper comfort and relief for the sick and wounded sufferers was felt, was the want of good nursing. To send out a band of skillful nurses was soon found to be one of the most essential of all supplies. But unless these were really skilled, more harm than good would certainly accrue; zeal, without experience, could effect little; and a bevy of incompetent or ill-organized nurses would prove an incumbrance, instead of an assistance. Now it was that a field was opened for the wider exercise of Miss Nightingale's genius and philanthropy; and now it was that her admirable abilities were secured for this great object in view.

At the request of the Right Hon. Sydney Herbert, Miss Nightingale at once accepted the proposal that she should undertake to form and control the entire nursing establishment for the British sick and wounded soldiers and sailors in the Crimea. Indeed, it is asserted, that by a strange coincidence — one of those coincidences arising out of urgent necessity felt and met at once — she had, herself, written to Mr. Herbert on the very same day, volunteering her services where they were so much needed. The task was one which involved sacrifices and responsibilities of formidable magnitude—the risk of her own life, the pang of separation from her family and friends, the certainty of encountering hardships, dangers, toils, and the constantly-recurring scene of human suffering amidst all the worst horrors of war, together with an amount of obstacle and difficulty in the carrying out of her noble work wholly incalculable. Few but would have recoiled from such a prospect; Miss Nightingale, however, met it with her own spirit of welcome for occasion to devote herself in the cause of humanity. Heroic was the firmness with which she voluntarily encountered her task; glorious was the constancy with which she persevered in and achieved it. The same force of nature which had enabled her quietly and resolutely to accumulate powers of consolation and relief for the behoof of her fellow-creatures, enabled her to persist steadily to the end, and carry out her high purpose with a success, holy as it was triumphant.

The history of her enterprise has been well written by the author of "World-Noted Women," and we shall present it in very nearly her own words, only correcting in points upon which additional light has been given, and relieving the narrative of the tedium of too minute detail. On Tuesday, the 24th of October, 1854, Miss Nightingale, accompanied by Rev. Mr. Bracebridge and his wife, and a staff of thirty-seven nurses, set out from England. On her way through France, she and her companions were received with the most respectful attention; hotel-keepers refusing payment for their accommodation, servants declining the customary fees, and all classes vying to show sympathy with their mission. On passing through the French metropolis, one of the Paris journals made a characteristic remark upon Miss Nightingale's appearance, which, coming from the source whence it did, was the extreme of intended compliment and interest. The paper observed that "her toilet was charming, and she was almost as graceful as a Parisienne." On the Friday following, Miss Nightingale and her companions embarked at Marseilles in the Vectis steamer, and, after a stormy passage, they reached Scutari on the 5th of November, just before the wounded in the action of Balaklava began to arrive. Five rooms which had been set apart for wounded general officers were, happily, unoccupied, and these were assigned to Miss Nightingale and her nurses, who, in appearance and demeanor, formed a strong contrast to the usual aspect of hospital attendants. Under such management the chaotic confusion of the vast hospital was quickly reduced to order: the wounded, before left for many hours unattended, now scarcely uttered a groan without some gentle nurse being at hand to adjust their pillow, and alleviate their discomfort; tears stood m the eyes of many a veteran while he confessed his conviction, that indeed the British soldier was cared for by his country, since ladies would leave the comforts and luxuries of home to come and tend him in his misery. Far from realizing the fears which had been entertained by officials, that this new addition to the staff of a military hospital would not work well. Miss Nightingale and her nurses were "never found in the way except to do good."

In the mean time the reports of the condition of the destitute suffering and dying soldiery had created universal sympathy in England. It produced a sort of spontaneous action. A subscription was set afoot, and in less than a fortnight the sum of £15,000 was sent into the Times office for the above purpose. The proprietors of that journal sent out a special commissioner, Mr. Macdonald, to administer this fund, from which thousands of shirts, sheets, stockings, flannels, quilted coats, and hospital utensils, besides large quantities of arrow-root, sago, sugar, tea, soap, wine, and brandy were supplied. Whenever, as after the battle of Inkermann, crowds of wounded arrived, there was feminine ministry at hand to tend them; and when medical stores failed or demand arose for articles not forthcoming, the Times commissioner supplied Miss Nightingale at once with what was needed, if it could be procured by money in the bazars or stores of Constantinople. This promptitude of Mr. Macdonald in seconding Miss Nightingale's exertions, deserves all praise; for it mainly enabled her to carry out the immediate requisites of her plan. His own excellent letters, written at the time, give a most vivid picture of the difficulties she had to contend with, in the shape of ill-contrived arrangements alone, besides other obstructions to her procedure. A rule of the service which required that articles — needed for present use — should be obtained from home through the commissariat, and a regulation which appointed that a "board" must sit upon stores already-landed, before they could be given out, will serve as instances to show what were the obstacles against which Miss Nightingale had to exert her energies of discretion and presence of mind. To comprehend the evils occasioned by such impediments, an extract from one of the nurse's letters will offer an example: "I know not what sight is more heart-rending, to witness fine-looking, strong young men worn down by exhaustion, and sinking under it, or others coming in fearfully wounded. The whole of yesterday was spent in sewing men's mattresses together, then in washing and assisting the surgeons to dress their wounds, and seeing the poor fellows made as comfortable as their circumstances would admit of after five days' confinement on board ship, during which time their wounds were not dressed. Out of the four wards committed to my charge, eleven men died in the night simply from exhaustion, which, humanly speaking, might have been stopped, could I have laid my hands on such nourishment as I know they ought to have had."

In the article of hospital clothing, the same deplorable effects resulted from the delay and confusion which existed before Miss Nightingale's remedial measures came into operation. The original supply of these articles, inadequate as it was, had long been reduced so low, that but for the purchases made with the money of the fund, and distributed through Miss Nightingale, a large proportion of the invalids must have been without a change of under-clothing, condemned to wear the tattered, filthy rags in which they were brought down from the Crimea. A washing contract existed, indeed, but it was entirely inoperative; and the consequence was, that not only the beds, but the shirts of the men were in a state foul and unwholesome beyond description. To remedy this, a house well supplied with water was engaged at the charge of the fund, close to the Barrack Hospital, where the clothing supplied by Miss Nightingale might be cleansed and dried. Her supervision had an eye for all needs; her experience had a knowledge for all that should be done; and her energy enabled her to have carried into effect that which she saw and knew ought to be effected.

In ten days after their arrival Miss Nightingale and her assistants fitted up a sort of impromptu kitchen, and from this hastily-constructed resource, eight hundred men were daily supplied with their respective needed quantities of well-cooked food, besides beef-tea in abundance. They who are acquainted with the plan of cookery pursued in barracks, where all a company's meat and vegetables are boiled in one copper, the portions belonging to messes being kept in separate nets, will know how that food is likely to suit the sickly appetite of a fevered patient, and how invaluable a system which provided the needful light diet, prepared with due quickness, as well as nicety, would be in hospital treatment. This was effected by Miss Nightingale's kitchen, even in its early operation, and it subsequently attained a degree of excellence productive of extensive benefit, scarcely to be estimated by those unacquainted with the importance of such details. Her extraordinary intelligence and capacity for organization showed itself in subordinate, as well as principal points of arrangement. In what might be called "housekeeping duties," she showed womanly accomplishment, no less than nice judgment. When the nurses were not needed at the bedsides of the sick and wounded, they were employed by her in making up needful articles of bedding and surgical requisites—such as stump-pillows for amputation cases. Not only was the laundry in excellent working order, but by the strong representation of Miss Nightingale, the dysentery wards were cleansed out, and general purification was made a diligently-regarded particular. During the first two months after her arrival, when there was no one else to act. Miss Nightingale was the real purveyor of those vast establishments—the hospitals at Scutari—providing what could not be obtained through the regular channels of the service, and especially from her kitchen, supplying comforts without which many a poor fellow would have died. Her name and benevolent services were the theme of frequent and grateful praise among the men in the trenches; and the remark was uttered that she made the barrack hospital so comfortable that the convalescents began to show a decided reluctance to leave it. Stores of shirts, flannel, socks, and a thousand other articles, which she and her nurses distributed; brandy, wine, and a variety of things, required at a moment's notice, and which could be procured from Miss Nightingale's quarters without delay or troublesome formality, rendered her the virtual purveyor for the whole of that period, during which she was avowedly the person in whose keeping rested not only the comfort, but the existence of several thousand sick and wounded soldiers. One of Mr. Macdonald's impressive sentences serves to paint the condition of the spot in which Miss Nightingale at that time drew breath. He says: "Wounds almost refuse to heal in this atmosphere; the heavy smell of pestilence can be perceived outside the very walls." In one of the last letters he wrote, before he was compelled, by failing health, to return to England, the Times commissioner bore the following earnest testimony to Miss Nightingale's excellence. It affords a beautiful picture of her in the midst of her self-imposed task of mercy and charity. These are his words: "Wherever there is disease in its most dangerous form and the hand of the spoiler distressingly nigh, there is that incomparable woman sure to be seen; her benignant presence is an influence for good comfort, even amid the struggles of expiring nature. She is a 'ministering angel,' without any exaggeration, in these hospitals; and as her slender form glides quietly along each corridor, every poor fellow's face softens with gratitude at the sight of her. When all the medical officers have retired for the night, and silence and darkness have settled down upon those miles of prostrate sick, she may be observed alone, with a little lamp in her hand, making her solitary rounds. The popular instinct was not mistaken, which, when she set out from England on her mission of mercy, hailed her as a heroine; I trust that she may not earn her title to a higher though sadder appellation. No one who has observed her fragile figure and delicate health, can avoid misgivings lest these should fail. With the heart of a true woman, and the manners of a lady, accomplished and refined beyond most of her sex, she combines a surprising calmness of judgment and promptitude and decision of character. . . . I confidently assert that, but for Miss Nightingale, the people of England would scarcely, with all their solicitude, have been spared the additional pang of knowing, which they must have done, sooner or later, that their soldiers, even in hospital, had found scanty refuge and relief from the unparalleled miseries with which this war has hitherto been attended."

The difficulties of Miss Nightingale's task were not only those arising out of its own appertaining perils and sacrifices, and those which resulted from official mismanagement, but she encountered much opposition springing from professional prejudices and jealousies. On their first arriving, so far from being welcomed, the advent of the nurses was looked upon as an evil, resented as an interference, and treated with tacit, if not open discountenance. At the best they were tolerated, not encouraged. Cabals were got up, ill feeling fostered, party differences disseminated and fomented. Passive resistance in every shape was resorted to, to prevent the installing of the nurses in the military hospitals. Against all this nothing but the exquisite tact, firmness, and good sense of Miss Nightingale could have prevailed.

Having proved herself a vigorous reformer of hospital misrule, she had to encounter the tacit opposition of nearly all the principal medical officers; her nurses were sparingly resorted to, even in the barrack hospital, while in the general hospital, the headquarters of one of the chief medical authorities, she held a very insecure footing. But the return of this person to England, the continued deficiency of the purveying, and the increasing emergencies of the hospital service, enabled Miss Nightingale to extend the sphere of her usefulness; and thus, together with her own admirably patient perseverance, she succeeded in having her nurses employed in their proper posts, and her own system established in perfect working order.

The results are briefly summed up. After she had introduced her system there and brought it into successful operation under her powerful will and genial presence, the mortality diminished, and during the last six mouths the mortality among the sick was not much more than among the healthy Guards at home, and during the last five months two-thirds only of what it was at home. In one sentence the world may read her devotion to her mission of army, medical, and sanitary reform: "I was never out of the hospitals," she says, "never out of the hospitals night or day."

The Hon. and Rev. Sydney Godolphin Osborne, in his deeply-interesting work upon Scutari and its hospitals, gives a description of Miss Nightingale, as she appeared exercising her vocation among the sick and dying. He says: "In appearance, she is just what you would expect in any other well-bred woman, who may have seen, perhaps, rather more than thirty years of life; her manner and countenance are prepossessing, and this without the possession of positive beauty; it is a face not easily forgotten, pleasing in its smile, with an eye betokening great self-possession, and giving, when she wishes, a quiet look of firm determination to every feature.

Her general demeanor is quiet, and rather reserved; still, I am much mistaken if she is not gifted with a very lively sense of the ridiculous. In conversation, she speaks on matters of business with a grave earnestness one would not expect from her appearance. She has evidently a mind disciplined to restrain, under the principles of the action of the moment, every feeling which would interfere with it. She has trained herself to command, and learned the value of conciliation toward others, and constraint over herself. I can conceive her to be a strict disciplinarian; she throws herself into a work, as its head—as such she knows well how much success must depend upon the literal obedience to her every order. She seems to understand business thoroughly. Her nerve is wonderful; I have been with her at very severe operations; she was more than equal to the trial. She has an utter disregard of contagion. I have known her spend hours over men dying of cholera or fever. The more awful to every sense every particular case, especially if it was that of a dying man, her slight form would be seen bending over him, administering to his ease in every way in her power, and seldom quitting his side till death released him."

Delightful is that intimation that Miss Nightingale gives token of being "gifted with a lively sense of the ridiculous."

Possessing the exquisite perception of the pathetic in existence which her whole career proclaims her to have, it would have been a defect in her nature, nay, a lack of the complete feeling for pathos itself, had she not betrayed a capacity for receiving humorous impressions. Humor and pathos are so nearly allied, in their source within the human heart, so mingled in those recesses whence spring human tears at the touch of sympathy, that scarcely any being deeply affected by mournful emotion, can remain insensible to the keen appeal that resides in a ludicrous idea.

Shakspeare, who comprehended to perfection every impulse of humanity, affords multitudinous illustrations of this close consociation of a sense of pathos and a sense of humor in the finest natures. That particular feature chronicled by Mr.

Osborne in his personal description of Miss Nightingale, is just the exquisite point, to our imagination, that crowns her admirable qualities. It accords with an intensely-beautiful account of her that was related by Mr. Sydney Herbert at a public meeting convened in Miss Nightingale's honor. He said an anecdote had been sent to him by a correspondent showing her great power over all with whom she came in contact. He read the passage from the letter, which was this: "I have just heard such a pretty account from a soldier, describing the comfort it was, even to see Florence pass. 'She would speak to one and to another, and nod and smile to as many more; we lay there by hundreds; but we could kiss her shadow as it fell, and lay our heads on the pillow again content.' What poetry there is in these men! I think I told you of another, who said:

'Before she came there was such cussin' and swearin'; and after that it was as holy as a church.' That consoling word or two, that gentle 'nod and smile' in passing, were precisely the tokens of sympathy that would come with such home-felt charm to those manly hearts from a face possessing the emotional expression which we can conceive it naturally to have, just the woman with just the countenance to exercise an almost magical moral influence over men's minds. We are told, eye-witnesses have averred, that it was singular to remark how, when men, frenzied, perhaps, by their wounds and disease, had worked themselves into a passionate refusal to submit to necessary operations, a few calm sentences of hers seemed at once to allay the storm; and the men would submit willingly to the painful ordeal they had to undergo." Noble being! Exactly that blended firmness and gentleness which makes a woman's nature so all potent in its beneficial ascendency over manhood. Rough, brave fellows, that would have resisted like iron any amount of men's persuasion, would melt at once into submission at a "few calm sentences" from those lips of hers. We can fancy the mouth, capable of smiles, or quivering with deepest feeling, compressed into resolute steadfastness, as it persuaded the men into reasonable acquiescence with what was for their good, while betraying the latent sympathy with their every pang.

Among all her anxieties, responsibilities, and more vital affairs, also, she found opportunity to attend to intellectual needs; for on one occasion, we find from a letter written in the camp before Sevastopol during the Spring of 1856, that "through the exertions of Miss Nightingale a considerable quantity of school material, such as maps and slates, was supplied to the schools." From her own stores she supplied books and games to cheer the dull hours of convalescence; and was foremost in every plan for affording the men harmless recreation. On her responsibility she advanced from the "Times Fund" the necessary sum for completing the erection of the Inkermann Cafe; she aided the active senior chaplain in establishing a library and school-room, and warmly supported him in getting up evening lectures for the men. She took an interest in their private affairs, and forwarded their little savings to their families in England at a time when there was no provision for sending home small sums; she wrote letters for the sick, took charge of bequests for the dying, and punctually forwarded these legacies of affection to relatives; she studied the comfort of those who recovered, and had a tent made to protect such of them as were permitted take the air from the searching rays of an Eastern sun — moreover, enduring the mortification of a refusal of the hospital authorities to have this tent put up. Her activity of intelligence was almost miraculous; one of its personal observers. Dr. Pincuffs, declares: "I believe that there never was a severe case of any kind that escaped her notice; and sometimes it was wonderful to see her at the bedside of a patient who had been admitted perhaps but an hour before, and of whose arrival one would hardly have supposed it possible she could already be cognizant."

Miss Nightingale would not hear of going back to England till the war was over; although her health and strength were so far impaired that when a yacht was placed at her disposal by Lord Ward to admit of her taking temporary change of air in sea excursions to recruit her for further work, she had to be carried down to the vessel carefully and reverently in the arms of the men, amidst their blessings and prayers for her speedy recovery. Her noble devotion had touched the hearts of her countrymen long before her work was completed, and the nation's gratitude could not be restrained from its eager desire to bestow some public token of acknowledgment toward a woman, who, they felt, had earned so imperative a title to their affectionate thanks.

A testimonial of some sort was agreed upon as the only means of exhibiting their unanimous feeling, and of permitting everyone to contribute their share in the offering. But of what was it to consist? Sums of money to a lady in affluent circumstances, would be futile; ornaments to one whose chosen sphere was by the bedside of the sick, the poor, and the dying, would be idle. Any gift to herself, who had given her most precious possessions, her time, her attentions, her sympathy to others, was not to be thought of. In the first place, it was like an attempt to reward that which was beyond reward; to pay for that which was a free donation, and, moreover. Miss Nightingale distinctly declined receiving any thing *for herself.* The only thing that remained, then, was to raise a fund for benevolent purposes, and to place it at her disposal, that she might approximate it according as her own philanthropic heart and admirable practical judgment should think best.

Public meetings were called, presided over by a prince of the blood royal, and one who had been a personal witness of Miss Nightingale's grand work in the East; and attended by peers, members of Parliament, and some of the highest men in professional repute. They debated the question of the proposed "Nightingale Fund" in the noblest spirit of consideration—consideration for the delicate feelings of her who was the object of this testimonial of a nation's gratitude, and consideration for those who were desirous of making this public proffer of their homage. It was decided that "a fund to enable her to establish an institution for the training, sustenance, and protection of nurses and hospital attendants" would be the best form for this National testimonial to take. This determination met her cordial and heart-felt approval.

And now the time approaches when her noble duty in the East came to a close, by the declaration of peace. The date of her intended return to England was kept a profound secret, out of dread of that publicity which she has ever carefully shunned. Not only were the day and the spot of her probable landing preserved unknown, lest the popular welcome that would have greeted her arrival should take place; but desirous of maintaining the strictest incognito, she refused the offer of a passage in a British man-of-war, and embarked on board a French vessel, passing through France by night, and traveling through her own country unrecognized, till she arrived at her own home in Derbyshire, on Friday, August 15, 1856. There was one gracious welcome that Miss Nightingale could not but accept, and that was from the royal lady who was the sovereign head of the army, which had so long been the especial object of Miss Nightingale's devoted care. A visit of some days at Balmoral, where the Queen was then staying, in highland seclusion and enjoyment, was spent by Miss Nightingale in the sunshine of kindly favor; being treated, during her sojourn there, with the most marked distinction by her Majesty and every member of the royal family.

Since her return home. Miss Nightingale's name has met the public ear only in the quiet deeds of practical goodness consistent with her whole career, or in the record of patient suffering, her constitution never having recovered its tone of health. The recent accounts of her failing strength render it quite probable that, before the public shall read these pages, Mercy's Missionary will have become Heaven's Angel.

In Florence Nightingale all the world glorifies a woman who embodies the principle of devotion, in the widest sense of the word; true devoutness to God — worshiping him by best service, in benefiting her fellow-mortals, and fervent consecration of herself to a high and immortal cause.

www.ingramcontent.com/pod-product-compliance
Lightning Source LLC
Chambersburg PA
CBHW031403040426
42444CB00005B/403